Ace Your Internet Research

Ann Graham Gaines

Enslow Elementary
an imprint of
Enslow Publishers, Inc.
40 Industrial Road
Box 398
Berkeley Heights, NJ 07922
USA

http://www.enslow.com

Enslow Elementary, an imprint of Enslow Publishers, Inc.

Enslow Elementary® is a registered trademark of Enslow Publishers, Inc.

Library of Congress Cataloging-in-Publication Data
Gaines, Ann.
  Ace your Internet research / Ann Graham Gaines.
      p. cm. — (Ace it! information literacy series)
  Summary: "Readers will learn what the internet is, and how to do effective
research while staying safe online"—Provided by publisher.
  Includes bibliographical references and index.
  ISBN-13: 978-0-7660-3392-4
  ISBN-10: 0-7660-3392-9
  1. Internet research—Juvenile literature. 2. Internet searching—Juvenile literature.
3. Internet—Safety measures—Juvenile literature. I. Title.
  ZA4228.G35 2009
  001.4'202854678—dc22
                              2008032351

Printed in the United States of America

10 9 8 7 6 5 4 3 2

To Our Readers:
We have done our best to make sure all Internet Addresses in this book were active and
appropriate when we went to press. However, the author and the publisher have no control over
and assume no liability for the material available on those Internet sites or on other Web sites
they may link to. Any comments or suggestions can be sent by e-mail to comments@enslow.com
or to the address on the back cover.

♻ Enslow Publishers, Inc., is committed to printing our books on recycled paper. The paper
in every book contains 10% to 30% post-consumer waste (PCW). The cover board on the outside
of each book contains 100% PCW. Our goal is to do our part to help young people and the
environment too!

Cover photo: iStockphoto.com/Artemis Gordon
Interior photos: Alamy/JupiterImages/BananaStock, p. 30; Alamy/Christopher Baines, p. 33;
Alamy/Blend Images, pp. 34, 39; Corbis, p. 8; Getty Images/Alex Mares-Manton/Asia Images, p. 14;
Getty Images/Kevin Cooley, p. 27; iStockphoto.com/Andres Peiro, pp. 3, 5, 10, 17, 25, 29, 31, 37;
iStockphoto.com/Kativ, pp. 7, 36; iStockphoto.com/Amanda Rohde, p. 12; iStockphoto.com/Mustafa
Deliormanli, p. 19 (monitor); iStockphoto.com/arlindo71, p. 20; iStockphoto.com/Christine Balderas,
p. 41 (top and bottom); Mary Francis McGavic, p. 19 (screenshot illustration); NASA, p. 18; Courtesy:
NOAA Fisheries, p. 40; Photo Edit/Dennis MacDonald, p. 24; Photo Edit/Michael Newman, p. 38;
Photolibrary.com/Scholastic Studio 10, p. 4; SuperStock/age fotostock, p. 6.

Contents

The Internet is an amazing tool at school and at home.

What Is the Web, Anyway?

Kids today are so lucky! Twenty years ago, when people wanted to find information, they had to read books and magazines or watch TV. Today we have a tool that's very powerful—and very fun to use. That's the World Wide Web! The World Wide Web lets us find information from—you guessed it—all over the world.

People talk about the World Wide Web all the time. But many of us don't know the difference between the Internet and the Web. The Internet is a huge collection of computers around the world. These computers are connected to each other. People use the Internet in many ways—writing e-mail, instant messaging, moving files from one place to another, and surfing the Web.

In order to surf the Web, you need a computer that's connected to the Internet. The Web is part of the Internet.

People use the Web all over the world.
This is an Internet café in China.

It is made up of an enormous group of files called Web sites. Today, there are hundreds of millions of Web sites. Anyone can create one. People—or groups of people— use them to share words, pictures, music, and movies.

You can visit the World Wide Web on any computer with Internet access. Computers can connect to the Internet in different ways. You might have heard of cable modems, DSL lines, and satellite connections. These are all ways to connect your computer to the Internet.

Besides Internet access, you will also need a Web browser. This software makes it possible to view Web sites on your screen, once you have connected to the Internet. Some popular Web browsers are Internet Explorer, Firefox, and Safari. People can get on the Web in many different places. They use computers at home, at a friend's home, at school, in libraries, and at Internet cafés.

Kids use the Web to send e-mail messages, to play games, or to create Web sites. They also use the Web to do research. Doing research means hunting for information.

Connect your computer to the Internet, and you'll have a world of information at your fingertips!

Online Safety

The World Wide Web can be a very fun place to explore. Unfortunately, it can also be dangerous, especially for kids. Many Web sites are just for grownups. If you find one of these, close the window right away! Web sites sometimes ask users to become a member of a group. If that happens, get help from an adult you trust. Also, never type your personal information into a Web site without getting permission from an adult. Personal information includes your name, age, address, phone number, e-mail address, photograph, and the name of your school.[1]

Most important, never agree to get together with someone you met online. Tell a parent or guardian immediately. People you meet on the Web might not be who they say they are.[2] As one Internet safety expert says, it's important always to think before you click.[3]

The Web can be a powerful research tool. It can help you write an essay, work toward a scout badge, enter a contest, or learn about your favorite sports team. At school, your class might use computers to complete a Web quest. A Web quest is an activity where students go online to hunt for information.[4] It's an online treasure hunt!

Web Access in My Town

Where can you use a computer? Do you have Internet access at home? Are there computers in your classroom? How about in your school library? Check out your public library, too! Use a chart like this to make a list of places where you can use the Web.

Name	Address	Phone Number	Open Hours
my house!	—	—	until bedtime
school library	42 Laurel Street	884-9270	school days 8 a.m.–4 p.m.

Wow! That's a Lot of Information!

Are you looking for information? You might want to head straight for the Web. Using the Web can be fun and easy. It gives you information as fast as the click of a mouse. Be careful, though—the Web is not always the right source for your research. John R. Henderson works in the library at Ithaca College in Ithaca, New York. He says, "An hour on the Web may not answer a question that you could find within two minutes of picking up a . . . book."[5] If you need simple information—such as basic facts about tornadoes—you can save time by going to a book. It could be a reference book, like an encyclopedia. Or it could be a nonfiction book like this one.

Other times, it's a better idea to look on the Web first. Why? One reason is that the Web has a whole lot of information. There are millions and millions of Web sites, and they're created all over the world.

Another reason to use the Web is that it can give you brand new information. It is constantly growing. Every day, new Web pages go up. People often update their Web pages by adding current information. It's up to you to check the facts—but you'll never find a bigger collection of them!

The Web can also be a starting point for *more* information. Let's say you are writing an essay about animal shelters. You can look up your local animal shelter on the Web and find an article by the director of the shelter. An article like this will probably answer lots of your questions.

A third reason to use the Web is that it has multimedia technology. Let's look at the word *multimedia* so we can understand what it means. *Multi* means "many." The word *media* means "a way to communicate information." So, multimedia technology is technology that uses lots of ways to communicate information. Web sites can combine words with pictures, sounds, animation, and videos. Let's say you're interested in otters, for example. On the Web, you could read about otters. Then you could look at photos of them, watch a video of them swimming, and hear the sounds they make—all on one site!

All Web sites have one thing in common: every site is assigned its own universal resource locator (URL). A URL is an address. If you know a Web site's URL, you can always find it. Just type the URL into the address line in a Web browser. Press the ENTER or RETURN button, and your browser will take you straight to that site.

There are many different kinds of Web sites. When you are doing research, you need to find informational Web sites. They give facts about one or more topics. Good informational Web sites are created by libraries, museums, schools, colleges, universities, government agencies, and

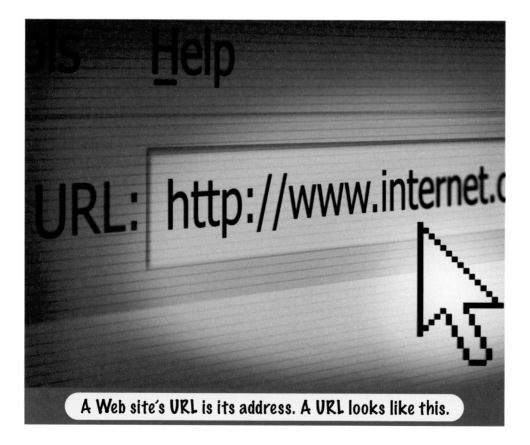

A Web site's URL is its address. A URL looks like this.

12

other organizations. Later in this book, you'll learn how to look at a Web site's address to find out what kind of site it is.

News sites are also helpful for researchers. These sites are created by newspapers, magazines, and television news stations. Some news sites include blogs. A blog is an online diary, journal, or source of news about a certain topic. Some journalists write blogs about their exciting experiences in the world.[6] Your library also has special databases with collections of news articles from years ago.

What if you want to do research about the history of your favorite candy? Business sites give you information about a company's product—whether it's a movie, a CD, or a type of chocolate candy. Some business sites are especially entertaining for kids. Just beware: businesses also use their Web sites to advertise their products to kids like you.

Personal Web sites are sites that individual people create. Warning! Be careful if you use a personal Web site. After all, anyone can put up a Web site. These sites are only helpful if the author knows a lot about a subject. If you're looking for reliable information, it needs to come from an expert. That's someone who has studied a subject for a long time. Later in this book, we'll discuss how to find out who created a Web site.

Web sites are made up of Web pages. These are a lot like the pages of a book. A Web site starts with a home page.

Ask the Expert!

What's one great thing about the Internet? It makes it much easier to contact experts. Many Web sites give you a chance to send a question to an expert. One example is NASA's "Human Space Flight Ask the Expert" page. Visit the page, and you can write to a member of a space shuttle crew.

The National Park Service also has a special page. You can write to a historian and ask a question about national parks or American history. For example, you could write to a National Park Service historian who works at a Civil War historic site.

If you find the right site, you can even write to an expert from another country!

This is the first page you see. Some home pages have a special feature called a site map. It shows you how the site is organized. Other home pages have a list of terms or bullets on the side or along the top. The items on this list are called hyperlinks, or links for short. A link is a word, a group of words, or a picture. Sometimes there are links in the middle of a paragraph, too. They are usually underlined or in a different color.

When you see a link, move your pointer over it with the mouse. Your pointer will probably turn into a hand. Then click on the link to see if it leads to another page. This new Web page might be part of the same Web site, or it could belong to a different site. Don't worry about getting lost. Web browsers have a special BACK button. It lets you return to the page you were on before.

Most Web pages have a title at the top. You'll also see some text at the bottom that says who created the Web site. Often you will see a date there. This tells you when the site was created or updated. Knowing a Web site's creator helps you decide whether you can trust the information.

Spotlight: National Geographic Kids

National Geographic Kids is a great Web site to help you learn how Web sites work. First, go to the home page. You will see many features in the middle of the page—articles, activities, and games. Look for the menu bar and the search box. Also look for the copyright statement. It says that this page was created by National Geographic. It tells you the date when it was created. Now start clicking on some links. It's fun to explore!

Before you start to do Web research, explore a few Web sites. This will help you understand how they're organized. Here are some suggestions for places to visit. The Library of Congress American Memory site has many interesting historical papers, photographs, and artifacts to look at. The National Aquarium's site has information about visiting the aquarium and tells you about the many sea creatures that live there. Author Beverly Cleary's Web site has lots of information about her very funny books. FunBrain is a site with a lot of games to play. As you look at these sites, compare their features. Take notes about them using the form below.

Web Site Information

Web site name: All About the Internet
Web site address: http://www.Web address goes here
Main purpose of the site (circle one) (information)/ education/entertainment/fun/advertising/personal site
Main links on the home page: About This Site, History, Using the Internet, Types of Web Sites, Internet for Kids
Special features (images? video?): photos, videos, music
Author/creator information: Internet Education Organization
Date of creation: 2009
Use for my project? (circle one) (Y) N

Start Your Search Engines!

The World Wide Web is huge. Using the Web is "a bit like trying to get a sip of water from an uncorked [open] fire hydrant."[7] It takes some skill to find what you want on the Web.

Here's the good news—plenty of people can help you learn to do research on the Web. For example, librarians are experts at searching for information. They know what you'll be able to find on the Web, and they can tell you how to find it. Your teachers and family members can help, too.

One good place to start your Web research is a search engine. A search engine is a Web site that helps you find information about the topic you choose. Some of the best search engines are Google.com and Yahoo.com. AskforKids.com is like a search engine. It's designed specially for kids.

Science on the Web

The World Wide Web is a wonderful place to do research about science. Let's say you're trying to understand how volcanoes  work. Science Web sites can offer more than a book can. You will find animation, videos, and lots of photos. Sites might also include games and activities that make learning fun.

There is another reason to do science research on the Web. Information is up-to-date. If you surf NASA's site (see picture from NASA at left) or Bill Nye the Science Guy, you'll find out about new discoveries. The information in a book might already be old news.

The key to good Web research is knowing what you want to find out. First, think about your topic. Brainstorm for a list of questions you'd like to answer. You can even read a bit to find out what's interesting about your topic. Once you've got a topic, you're ready to choose keywords for your Web research. Keywords are words that work like a key. They open up the door that leads you to the information you need.

Sometimes your keywords will be obvious. Maybe you're looking for information about cobras. *Cobra* will be your main keyword. Other times, your search is more complicated. Let's say you want to learn about soccer in the United States. The keyword *soccer* is too broad. If you use it, you'll get too many Web sites that have to do with soccer. However, if you use the keywords *soccer team USA*, the sites you get will match your topic.

Keyword Search on a Search Engine

Keywords can be too broad, but they can also be too narrow. If you want to know all about marsupials, the keyword *kangaroo* won't give you enough information. There are lots of different marsupials—not just kangaroos.

Once you have a list of keywords, you're ready to start your Web search. Search engines are easy to use. Begin by typing the search engine's URL into your Web browser. Then look for a big blank box on the page. This box is often marked SEARCH. Type your keywords in the box and press ENTER. (If you're looking for an exact phrase, put it in quotation marks, like this: "skateboard grips.") In just a few seconds, the computer will show you a list of Web sites. For each site, you'll see a name

How Search Engines Work

How do search engines work? They send out "spiders"! These are tools that make lists of words from Web sites. The search engine figures out which sites include each word most often. When you do a search, the search engine comes up with Web sites that use your keywords in many places. This is your results list.

Idea Map

An idea map helps you come up with ideas for keywords. The research topic goes inside the center circle. In the outside circles are keywords to use in your search for information.

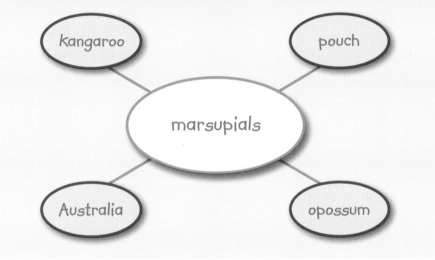

and a short description. Scroll down to see more of the list. It might go on for several pages.

Read some of the Web site descriptions. Do you think they will be helpful? Click on some of the links and visit the sites. If you don't see the information you want, do your search again. First, check to see if you spelled your keywords correctly. If that's not the problem, add another keyword—or change your keywords completely.

Model Keyword Search

Imagine that a class is learning about endangered animals. One student does Web research to find out more about the Ridley sea turtle.[8]

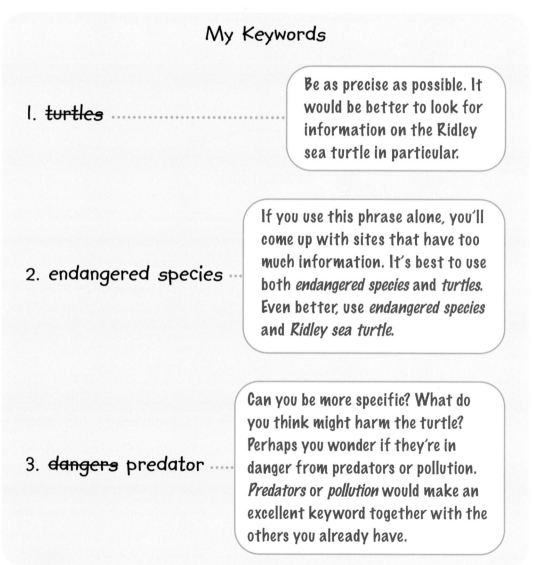

My Keywords

1. ~~turtles~~ .... Be as precise as possible. It would be better to look for information on the Ridley sea turtle in particular.

2. endangered species ... If you use this phrase alone, you'll come up with sites that have too much information. It's best to use both *endangered species* and *turtles*. Even better, use *endangered species* and *Ridley sea turtle*.

3. ~~dangers~~ predator ... Can you be more specific? What do you think might harm the turtle? Perhaps you wonder if they're in danger from predators or pollution. *Predators* or *pollution* would make an excellent keyword together with the others you already have.

22

The same student revised, or changed, her list of keywords. These keywords will make her search more successful:

Revised Keywords List

1. Ridley sea turtles
AND . . .
2. endangered species
3. predators
4. pollution

It's a good idea to combine your keywords. You can do this by adding the word *and* between them. This way, you'll come up with information not just about the sea turtle, but about why it's endangered.

You can find many types of information on the World Wide Web. This boy is searching for photographs.

Pictures, Movies, Music—and More

The Web is a great place to find information in many different forms. On Web sites you can find more than just written descriptions (text). You'll also see images—photographs, paintings, illustrations, diagrams, charts, and maps. Many sites include sound, video, and animation.

Let's talk about images first. Why might you want to find an image? Maybe you are trying to understand the difference between a sand bar shark and a sand tiger shark. Boy, would a photo help! An illustration would also be great to include in your research presentation. (If you take an image from a Web site, you have to get permission. More on that later in this book.)

You can find images with a search engine. Many search engines let you search for only images. For example,

Google has a special images search page. You get there from the home page by using the IMAGES link. Type in your keywords—for example, *sand tiger shark*. Hit ENTER or click the SEARCH button. On the results page you will see thumbnails. These are photos so small that dozens fit on a single page. Click on a thumbnail you would like to use. Have an adult help you save, e-mail, or print it.

There are other ways to find pictures. Museums and organizations like NASA and the Library of Congress have image galleries on their Web sites. These galleries work like smaller versions of a search engine.

You might also want to do a Web search for videos. Maybe you've heard about a trick that a biker performed at the X Games. Or perhaps your grandmother told you about watching an astronaut walk on the moon in 1969. There are two ways to find videos. You could use your search engine's special video search page. Another way is to add the word *video* to your keyword search.

What about audio? You can go online to look for music. Look for a record company Web site and listen to samples. Then ask your parents if you can buy songs at an online music store like iTunes. If you like a specific band, use a search engine to see if they have an official Web site and songs to download. You can also find speeches and other audio files on the Web.

26

This boy is using headphones to listen to audio clips on the Internet.

It is possible to download pictures, music, and videos from the Web onto your computer. Remember, though, that it's not always safe to do so. Some file-sharing Web sites are illegal. Always ask permission from a trusted adult before downloading.

Understanding Copyright

When an author writes a book, she is granted a copyright. That means she is the legal owner of what she has written. If other people want to use her words, they have to get her permission. The same is true for art and music. That's why it's wrong for individuals to put copies of songs onto file-sharing sites.

To practice doing a Web search, look for information about a movie you really like. In the first column, write the URL and name of a Web site that tells you about the movie in words (text). In the second column, write down a site that has pictures of the movie's stars. In the third column, write the name and address of a site that lets you play one of the movie's songs. In the last column, write a site where you saw a video clip from the movie. (See the next page for an example.)

28

Text	Pictures	Music	Video
Movie Summaries 2009: http://www.Web address goes here	Universal Movie Stills: http://www.Web address goes here	Once Upon a Soundtrack: http://www.Web address goes here	Famous Comedies Online: http://www.Web address goes here

The list below is an example of all the different kinds of media you can use for your research.

My Ridley Sea Turtle Sources

1. Galveston County Daily News, "Sea Turtles Making a Comeback in Texas," May 2, 2008, http://www.Web address goes here

2. Kemp's Sea Turtle WebQuest, Sea Turtle Digital and Video Gallery, no date, http://www.Web address goes here

   video of turtle swimming in aquarium

3. National Geographic, Kemps-ridley Sea Turtle 1996–2008 http://www.Web address goes here

   has a great photo and a map

4. Texas Parks and Wildlife, Kemp's Ridley Sea Turtle April 11, 2007 http://www.Web address goes here

   a great source for facts

Some Web sites are better than others. Carefully explore each site to see if you can trust the facts it gives you.

5

Is This Site Any Good?

Here is the good news: as you do Web research, you'll find lots of Web sites. Now the bad news: they're not all going to be helpful! You can run into all kinds of problems when you're doing research on the Web. Some sites won't be useful. They won't have the information you need. Worse yet, they might not be reliable. In other words, they might not tell you the truth!

How can you tell which Web sites will be good to use for your project? You need to evaluate them. That means you decide whether they are valuable and reliable. What does that mean? Why wouldn't a Web site be reliable? Remember, anyone in the world can create a Web site. Some people put wrong information on the Web on purpose, perhaps as a joke. Sometimes a site is not reliable because the author does not understand the topic.

Sometimes you won't have to worry about the value of a site. If your parent, teacher, or librarian recommends a certain site, it's probably reliable. If you find a site on your own, you can ask an adult if it's a good one. Or, you can try judging for yourself whether a Web site is good. Ask yourself these questions: Does it give the name of the person or organization who made the site? Does it say when the Web site was created? Was the site created by a school or a museum? If you can answer yes to all these questions, it's probably a good site.

Whatever sites you use, take time to double-check the facts. In most cases, you should find more than one source. Even excellent sites can't provide all the facts on any one topic. They will miss some information.

Go through these steps when you find a new Web site.[9] First, look at its title to figure out its topic. Next, check to see who created it. The URL extension can give you a clue. The extension of a URL is the group of letters at the end, after the period (dot). If the extension is *.edu*, the site comes from a school. Another abbreviation is *.com*, for *commercial*. That means a business has put up the Web site. If you see *.org*, that stands for *organization* (like a museum or a church). Government Web sites end in *.gov*. American sites end in three letters. Sites created outside the United States end in a two-letter abbreviation—*.ca* for Canada, *.uk* for the United Kingdom, *.jp* for Japan, and so on.

Books on the Web

Do you love to read? You can use the World Wide Web to find out more about books. The American Library Association's Great Web Sites for Kids page lists sites about favorite authors and illustrators. You'll also find suggestions about new books to read. There are even stories for you to read right on the Web.

There's a lot to do besides look at the extension. It's best if you figure out *exactly* who created a site. This isn't always going to be possible, but you should try. Look at the bottom of a Web page. There you might see the name of an author or an organization. You also might find copyright information, or even an About Us page.

Also try to find out when the page was created. That information is not always available. But it's important if you need current information—for example, if you're trying to find out about the latest scientific research or a new hip-hop hit. Other times, the date won't really matter. Just remember, though, that old Web sites might not have accurate information.

Creating Web Pages

Have you ever thought about creating your own Web page? Many very cool sites have been created by kids. Young authors use their sites to share information about their hobbies and interests. If you're interested in creating a Web

page, you'll first need to get permission from an adult at school or at home. An adult can help you make a Web site safely. After you have permission, decide what to put on your site. Write some text. Collect pictures (don't forget to get permission to use them, if they're not yours). Then go to the library to check out a book, or look for a Web site that explains how to create a Web page.

Evaluating a Web Site

Use a checklist like this one to evaluate the Web sites you visit. It will help you decide whether the source is accurate and helpful.[10]

What is the address of the Web site? (The address usually starts with *http://www.*)

Check *Yes* or *No.*	Yes	No
Is the spelling correct?	☑	☐
Is the author's name and e-mail address on the page? (This could be a person or an organization.)	☑	☐
Are the links easy to find?	☑	☐
Are the words easy to read?	☐	☑
Is there a date that tells you when the page was made?	☑	☐
Do the photographs look real and professional?	☐	☑
Do the photographs on the site help you learn about the topic?	☑	☐
Does the site tell you who took the photographs?	☐	☑
Does the title tell you what the site is about?	☑	☐
Does the site answer some of your research questions?	☑	☐
Does the author of the page say things that you know are wrong?	☐	☑
Does the author include a bibliography (a list of the sources he or she used to make the Web site)?	☐	☑

35

Does this stack of books look scary? The Internet has an *unlimited* stack of information! Learn how to keep track of it.

Using What You Find

Doing Web research can be a lot of fun. It can also be very frustrating. If you are not careful, you can lose track of some great information. Imagine that you're on one perfect Web page. It has the list of fascinating facts that you need for your school report. Then you follow a link to another Web page—and then another and another. Now you're lost! You can't get back to those fascinating facts.

How can you keep this from happening? There are two ways you can look back at the Web sites you've visited. If you haven't quit your Web browser yet, you can use the BACK or ◀ button. Now, let's say you already quit your Web browser, but you're still using the same computer. Open the browser back up. Click on the HISTORY button to see a list of every site you've been to recently. Phew!

How can you keep track of the Web sites you like? Some kids use the same computer over and over again. Your family might own one. Or you might have a computer you often use at your school, a library, or a youth center. If that's the case, you can create bookmarks or favorites using the Web browser. That means you'll add the Web site's title to a list. In the ADD TO FAVORITES or BOOKMARK dialogue box, you can see what name the site will be saved under (you can change that if you want to). Whenever you open the Web browser, you can go to your

You can print out the information on a Web page if you want to use it later.

Taking notes is another way to save
information you find on the Internet.

list of bookmarks or favorites. Select the title of the Web
site you like, and the browser will take you right there.

What if you want to use the information you found on
the Web when you're not connected to the Internet? You
can print out the Web pages you like. Before you do so, use
the PRINT PREVIEW command (under the File menu) to
see what you'll actually be printing out. Printing is an
excellent idea if you want to look at an entire Web page
later. On the other hand, you might waste a lot of paper.
Only print what you really need.

You can also take notes from Web sites. Make sure
to record the URL, the name of the site, the date it was

created or updated, and the date you visited it. Also take notes on the interesting information you have found. You could make your notes in a word processing program, in a notebook, or on note cards. There is one very important thing to remember while taking notes. Never write information word for word unless you put it in quotation marks. If you use someone else's words without quotation marks, you are plagiarizing (see "Avoiding Plagiarism" on page 42).

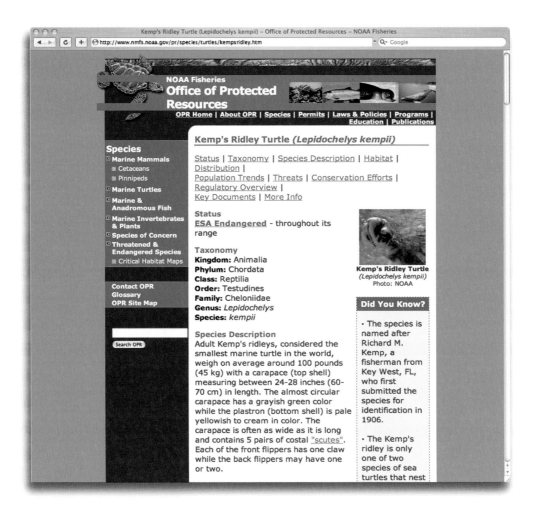

My Notes: NOAA Source on Kemp's Ridley Turtles

Adult Kemp's ridleys, considered the smallest marine turtle in the world, weigh on average around 100 pounds (45 kg) with a carapace (top shell) measuring between 24–28 inches (60–70 cm) in length. almost circular carapace has a grayish green color

plastron (bottom shell) is pale yellowish to cream in color.

carapace is often as wide as it is long and contains 5 pairs of costal "scutes."

These notes are terrible. They copy the exact words of the author! This is plagiarism.

Ridley = smallest turtles that live in the sea

Average weight—100 pounds

Top shell (carapace) 24–28 inches long, circle-shaped

On top—grayish green

Underneath—cream to yellow

These notes are much better. They are short, and the student uses her own words.

As the years go by, you will probably do a lot more Web research. At first, you might feel like you don't know what to do. Don't worry! Over time you will gain skill. Your Web research will get better and better. You'll also find more and more ways to use this skill. Web research can help you write great stories and reports, put together interesting presentations, and find out more about your hobbies and interests. Enjoy!

Avoiding Plagiarism

What is plagiarism? That's when you do not write your paper all by yourself. Instead, you use other people's work without saying so. This can happen if you're not very careful when you take notes. Never copy exact sentences from a source—unless you see something that you want to quote. If you do quote someone else's words, use quotation marks around the words. Write the name of the person who said them. For example, write, "Animal expert Bob Feinberg says, 'Always make sure your parakeet has enough water.'" Finally, make sure to include the source of the quote in your bibliography.

Teachers see plagiarism as a serious problem. If your teacher thinks you have plagiarized without understanding why it is wrong, she might let you redo your work. But many teachers will give your paper a very low grade or a zero.

Use a form like this to record your own important information for your bibliography.

URL: http://www.Web address goes here	
Title: Ridley Turtle Center	
Date created: 2008	
Date you used the site: Jan. 8, 2009	

Glossary

access—The ability to get information from a source, such as a computer or a book.

bibliography—A list of sources used in a paper or other research project.

blogs—Online journals.

broad—Wide-ranging; including many topics.

database—A large collection of information.

evaluate—To make a decision about how valuable or correct something is.

extension—A dot (period) plus the last two or three letters at the end of a URL—i.e., *.gov, .edu, .com.*

home page—The first page you see when you enter the main URL for a Web site.

hyperlinks—Words or images on a Web site that lead to a new location, such as another Web site, when you click on them.

illegal—Against the law.

Internet—A worldwide system of networked, or linked, computers.

keywords—Words or phrases that you use to begin a search on the Web.

multimedia—Using more than one way to display information at a time—for example, mixing words with photographs, music, and video.

narrow—Limited; having few choices.

network—A group of objects that are linked together.

plagiarizing—Taking the work of someone else and presenting it as your own.

reference book—A book that contains facts about general topics or words, like a dictionary or an encyclopedia.

reliable—Trustworthy.

research—A search for information about a certain topic.

samples—Small parts of songs or other sound files.

scroll—To move up and down on a computer screen.

search engine—A Web site that finds sources with information about a certain topic, based on a keyword search.

source—Material that provides information, such as a book, magazine, song, Web site, piece of art, or interview with a person.

surfing—Exploring the World Wide Web by going from one site to another.

thumbnails—Photographs that are about the size of a grownup's thumbnail.

URL—A Web site address.

Web browser—A computer program that allows users to surf the Internet, such as Internet Explorer or Firefox.

Web site—A collection of Web pages that is reached through an introductory or home page.

World Wide Web—A network of documents (also known as sites) that are available on the Internet.

Chapter Notes

1. PBS Kids, "Get Your Web License," 1995–2008 <http://pbskids.org/license/index.html> (March 15, 2008).

2. Larry Magrid, "My Rules for Online Safety," *SafeKids.com*, 2004–2005 <http://www.safekids.com/kidsrules.htm> (February 29, 2008).

3. Parry Aftab, "ThinkB4UClick: How To avoid doing something stupid online," *Xanga Safety*, May 22, 2006 <http://safety.xanga.com/2006/05/22/thinkb4uclick/> (March 1, 2008).

4. WebQuest Direct, "What Is a WebQuest?" 2008 <http://www.webquestdirect.com.au/whatis_awq.asp> (October 10, 2008).

5. John R. Henderson, "Make Sure You Are in the Right Place," *ICYouSee: T Is for Thinking*, modified January 27, 2006 <http://www.ithaca.edu/library/training/think1.html> (March 16, 2008).

6. Merriam-Webster, *Merriam-Webster Online*, 2007–2008 <http://www.merriam-webster.com/dictionary/blog> (March 17, 2008).

7. Alexander Colhoun, "But—I Found It on the Internet!" *Christian Science Monitor*, April 25, 2000 <http://www.csmonitor.com/2000/0425/p16s1.html> (March 17, 2008).

8. Elisa Magee and Linda Miller, "Kemp's Ridley Sea Turtle WebQuest," *Blattman Elementary School*, January 2004 <http://www.nisd.net/blattman/links/4/sea_turtle/1_kemps_ridley_webquest.htm> (December 4, 2008).

9. Cheap WebHosting Directory, "Why Website Title Tags Are So Important," 2008 <http://www.cheaphostingdirectory.com/art-why-website-title-tags-are-so-important-29.html> (March 17, 2008).

10. Kathleen Schrock, "Critical Evaluation of a Web Site, Elementary School Level," *Kathy Schrock's Guide for Educators*, 2006 <http://school.discoveryeducation.com/schrockguide/pdf/evalelem.pdf> (August 31, 2008).

Further Reading

Books

Amihud, Zohar. *Look Mom! I Built My Own Website.* Fords, N.J.: BookChamp, 2005.

Hawthorne, Kate and Daniela Sheppard. *Young Person's Guide to the Internet: An Essential Website Reference Book for Young People, Parents, and Teachers.* New York: Routledge Falmer, 2005.

Levete, Sarah. *Keeping Safe.* Mankato, Minn.: Stargazer Books/The Creative Company, 2007.

Parks, Peggy J. *The Internet.* Detroit: Lucent Books, 2006.

On the Internet

Multnomah College Library: Evaluating websites
http://www.multcolib.org/homework/webeval.html

PBS Kids: Get Your Web License
http://pbskids.org/license/index.html

Ramapo Catskill Library System: KidsClick!
http://www.kidsclick.org/

Other Helpful Web Sites

Below you will find the URLs of the helpful Web sites mentioned in this book.

http://spaceflight.nasa.gov/feedback/expert/
http://www.nps.gov/history/history/askhist.htm
http://kids.nationalgeographic.com/
http://memory.loc.gov/ammem/index.html
http://www.aqua.org/
http://www.beverlycleary.com
http://www.funbrain.com/
http://www.nasa.gov
http://www.billnye.com
http://www.google.com
http://www.ala.org/greatsites

Index